Poetry
of
Life

GLENDA JENSEN

ISBN   978-1-966473-56-5 Ebook
ISBN   978-1-966473-55-8 Paperback

The EC Publishing LLC books may be ordered
through booksellers or by contacting:

EC Publishing LLC
116 South Magnolia Ave.
Suite 3, Unit F
Ocala, FL 34471, USA
Direct Line: +1 (352) 644-6538
Fax: +1 (800) 483-1813
http://www.ecpublishingllc.com/

Ordering Information:
Quantity sales. Special discounts are available on quan-
tity purchases by corporations, associations, and others. For
details, contact the publisher at the address above.

Printed in the United States of America

Table of Contents

Shout Outs

I strongly give shout outs to my family, my tenth grade teacher who gave her classes an assignment concerning writing a poem, and all my former students. This was the beginning of my gift of writing.

Family

Forty years ago

Forty years ago, you were born
After 14 hours of labor and cussing the nurse
Your cries were finally heard
And I knew that a son was born

As you grew into a toddler
You immediately let your personality shine
You were independent yet funny
I marveled at your first haircut
I used to laugh at your mischievousness
And adore the hugs you gave

When you reached elementary school
Your athleticism proved to be authentic
Remember only six years old
And playing for The Cowboys
Baseball was also your favorite game
Even though your team did not win much

Approaching middle school
You discovered the trumpet and was in the band
You often threatened to play revile
I would pray that you would not
But alas one day the horn became broken
And so ended your band career

High School was a whole new world
You shined in football playing defense and offense
You suffered a concussion and a separated shoulder
My! How I wanted to comfort you
But held back as so not to embarrass you
I remember the last game when seniors were honored
I was proud

The college years seemed to fly by fast
I remember the day you became an Aggie alumnus
I knew your PaPa would have beamed with pride
As you walked the stage and received your diploma
I knew that you would go far
And yet here you are

Forty years have gone by like a flash
But you still show the young heart in you
You have grown into a fine young man
With a nose for success
Whether it be in life or at work

(Dedicated to my son, Michael Glen Hill)

My Daughter, My Friend

From diapers to heels
From short hair to long
From blue jeans to dresses
From a cute baby to a beautiful woman
You have always been my sweet angel

Before you were born
I knew you were to be a girl
And when the doctor told me
All I could say is "I Know"

From babyhood into being a toddler
You were always a sick little girl
But Almighty God and his angels persevered
And made you well again

From playing soccer at five
To playing basketball in high school
You were always strong
Size was never an issue

Approaching middle school
You discovered the clarinet
But 'some' notes were not your forte'
So percussion became your passion

High school was a whole new world
You excelled at everything
Whether it being an athlete or on the drill team
All was good upon graduation

The first year at Sam Houston State
Proved to be promising
But the Air Force called your name
So off you went into the Wild Blue Yonder

Years have come and gone
And there were obstacles in the way
But you surmounted them
Like hurdles at a track meet

Being a mom and daughter
Are your best two traits
You have a nose for achievement
Whether you are running, working, or cheering at a game

Forty years have gone by like a flash
But you still show the young heart in you
You survived cancer while you laughed at it in the face
You have grown into a fine young woman

(Dedicated to my daughter, Kristina Leigh Hill Canales)

Wife, Mother, Teacher, Daughter

In your world, you wear many hats
Not to mention the many that wil yet to be
You started out small and strong
As you grew, you became independent
However, you are still being confident

When you were born and looked up at me
I knew that you were destined to be successful
As you grew, nothing seemed to deter your motivation
Your self-confidence and self-esteem grew
Into a strong, beautiful young woman

As you grew, you independence really shined
Sure there were pitfalls and obstacles
But you figuratively got up and brushed off
The negativity that life plunged at you
You stared down the evilness
And stood up proud and successful

One of many of the positives in your life
Was when you became a bride
Yes, you married the love of your life
He has strengthened you even more
To stretch into the woman you have become
He is truly your prince as you are his princess

The most delightful of your time here on earth
Was when you became a mother, mom, mommy
Your true self and personality really shown forth
Your babies, no matter how old, designates your personality
You are kind, supportive, and a real trooper
When it comes to your children

Speaking of children, I see the light
When you speak of your profession, your life goal
Teacher is a word that can transform across the ages
Being a teacher myself makes me smile
When I know that you are one yourself
After all, the children of today
Shall be our legacy of tomorrow

Proud is the word that comes to mind
When I think of you and what you have molded into
The kind of person that you have become
Makes me want to shot to the world
"She's my daughter, and I'm proud as punch"
Continue on the path that God has chosen
And you will only shine even more.

(Dedicated to my daughter, Desire'e Lynn Dulong Stone}

Grandchildren and Grandparents

Those precious smiles and laughs
Big eyes looking up waiting for guidance
Small hands folded in prayer
All this and more tugs at our hearts

Whether playing football with the boys
Or playing tea party with the girls
We're glad to do it; we want to do it
Because that's what grandparents do

Baking cookies, eating M&Ms, or riding bikes
Brings youth back into the life of a grandparent
Watching cartoons and Disney movies all night
Only produce love and gladness of the time

But wait; sometime there are tears
From a hurt finger or a bf/gf problem
Whose shoulder is available?
Grandma or Grandpa is there to pick up the pieces

Through the coos, the tantrums, the smiles
The laughs, the anger, and the tears
The voice of a grandparent
Shall always be there for their grandchildren

Who Is This Woman

Her face was the first one you saw
The first embrace belonged to her
She kissed all the boo-boos of life
And taught you how to pray

She made all your lunches everyday
As you traveled through elementary school
Until one day you were able to buy those lunches
But it was she who paid for them

She took you shopping for all your clothes
Including your first prom dress or suit
Then graduation came quickly
As you walked the stage, her tears flowed like a river

When you went to college or the military
To begin your own steps of life
Your goodbye hugs could be felt for months
Upon completion of your task, you silently said "thank you"

Then a wedding needed planning
She was there to put things together
The cake was made; dresses or tuxes to be bought
The "I dos: were said; again tears

When you started a family of your own
She was the first to babysit
Who was this person
Who prayed when things went wrong

Who was this person?
Who God has given to you
Who gave you that first smile
You simply but honorably call her MOTHER

My Hero, My Buddy, My Dad

Fighting during World War II
No question he's my hero
Teaching me to ride a bike and drive a car
Yes, he's my hero
Crying on his shoulder when dates went bad
Definitely he's my hero

Watching Texas A&M football on Saturday
Then the Cowboys on Sunday
We were definitely buddies
Several times he took me to see a game
Glad to call him "Buddy"
Answered questions about how a car ran
So happy he was my buddy

Walking me down the aisle
On my wedding day
When five years later
Found me crying on his shoulder again
Due to the first divorce ever in our family
So pleased he was my Daddy

Whether hero, buddy, or Dad
He was always there with and for me
Having answers that I didn't have
Hero, buddy, AND Dad
He is missed and
Will be forever in my heart

In Remembrance

Grief

Drowning in a sea of tears
Since you left me
Seems like an eternity
With each and every day
I reach out of you
And you are not there
I say your name
But you do not answer
My ears long for your voice
My eyes look for your face
Then reality sinks in
And more tears are present

Celebration of Delbert Roland Binkley

His eyes would crinkle
When he smiled or laughed
He touched the hearts of many children
And was a magnet to ALL dogs
He was the man to call
When help or a favor was needed
His love of eagles
Was as big as his heart
He loved to see them soar in the sky
Just like his love for our Lord Jesus Christ
Mowing was his escape and passion
It gave him time to think and pray
His heart and kindness
Touched many people
Forever he will be missed
Forever he will be in our hearts
So, dear Delbert, here's a salute,
Many hats off to you, and
A glorious wave just to say,
"So long, 'til we meet again"

(Dedicated to my late husband, Delbert Roland Binkley)

Guitar Man

Reaching for his guitar
Brings to light a special bond
Music runs in his soul
A gift given by God

All of a sudden
Sounds are heard
But it is not noise
But an angelic sound

The man becomes
One with his guitar
The music together
Is of man and God

Guitars are his passion
But God is his director
Music is his love
But God puts it there

Love can be felt
When he plays
And is shared with others
As he plays from his heart

(Dedicated to Clay Armstrong, a special friend)

Ode to Rigo Canales

His heart was as big as the outdoors

His love for dogs was his passion

As he looked into the eyes of his loved ones

His love would climb even higher

No one can ever forget the sparkle in his eyes

As he brought laughter into everyone's life

This man of God will be missed but never forgotten

The love for this man will be forever and ever

(Dedicated to Rigo Canalas, my late son-in-law)

Patriotism

9-11 Remembered

Where were you when the planes crashed
Were you in an office or sitting in class
What were you thinking when those people died
Were you shocked, stunned, or did you sit down and cry

Uncle Sam bowed his head; Mother Liberty just cried
As she watched smoke fill the skies
Sam started shouting; Mom got mad
Fists started shaking at the men who were bad

The firemen stood and looked at the sight
What they saw gave them such a fright
One, two, three, four jets it did take
To cause the earth to feel such a quake

People of the world cried on that day
Then smiled knowing that those men will pay
Loved ones were saved; some were lost
Too much the price, too much the cost

Pride here in America? Yes, we got it
So much so, our enemies won't forget it
We are home of the brave and true
I've got pride; how about you?

Salute to Our Military

Standing in line
Waiting for that hair cut
Anxious about that call of Duty
Soldiers of the past
Who fought with courage and pride
For our freedom
Are never forgotten
Some came home
While others forfeited their lives
And others not clear in the mind
Whether WWI, WWII, Korea
Vietnam, Iraq, or Afghanistan
These brave soldiers
Will be heroes forever in our hearts

Thank a Veteran
November 11

A Salute to Our Veterans

By Glenda Jensen

My Dad fought in World War II
And grandpa served in ONE
A few friends went to Nam
While others saw the Storm and Iraq
Some came home to ticker-tape parades
Some just came home
While others just didn't come back
We salute you, our Veterans of red, white, and blue
For your courage, pride, and grace
Without your bravery running true
No choices we would make
We salute you, our Veterans, past and present
Not just this day but every day
Go forth, our brethren, and hold your heads high
We salute you, the brave, the proud, the true

Memorial Day Remembered

We salute you, our fallen brethren
To you we all say thanks
For without your bravery so true
Freedom would be captive in chains

There were Dads who fought in World War Two
And Grandpas who fought in One
Others were killed in Korea and Vietnam
While others fell in Iraq or Desert Storm

Our hats are off as we look to the heavens
And our thoughts are gathered as one
Silently, we beseech our God
And hope that peace will finally be won

Your courage will never be forgotten
Your prowess will be forever true
We will always remember those who fell
And gave their lives for the red, white, and blue

Holidays

Thanksgiving

Turkey and dressing – yummy, yummy, yummy

Have some pie – good for the tummy

Ask Uncle Rich to pass the potatoes

Now how about some salad loaded with tomatoes

Kindly bow your heads as we silently pray

Saying a special thanks on this special day

Give Cousin Mike another piece of cake

Is there any food left for me to take

Various foods are all on the table

I'm so full, but I'll try to move if I'm able

Nap time during the football game is a plan

Grabbing some hugs from grandpa and gran

Thanksgiving at Granny's House

Walking into Granny's dining room
Looked like being in a five star hotel
The table cloth had been ironed and neatly placed
Barely enough room for plates and silverware
Mumbles could be heard as the food was placed
Yummy does not explain it
Sitting around the table
Holding hands with each other
Sharing what we're thankful for
Then prayer was said to give grace
Grandpa did the carving
From Turkey to Ham ----But wait!
That's not all!
Then came dressing, gravy, potato salad, and mashed taters too
Don't forget deviled eggs and stuffed celery, as well
But the best part of the evening
Included Granny's special dessert table
German Chocolate cake, Pumpkin pie, and cupcakes too
So no more waiting --- Let's Eat!

Christmas is around the corner

w**H**ile having fun shopping

Reindee**R** prancing around anxiously

I can't wait to open presents

Ho! Ho! Ho! **S**ays Santa Claus

While **T**aking off in his sleigh

Chim**M**ney sliding is his sport

Also eating cookies and hot cocoa

Soooo, Merry Christmas to all and to all a Good night

Christmas

Happy Birthday, Jesus
That's what it's all about
Not gifts or Santa
Nor lights and decorations

Happy Birthday, Jesus
Thank You for Your gifts
Along with Your blessings
And many prayers answered

Happy Birthday, Jesus
Let us remember why You came
And celebrate Your love
With the grace of Your forgiveness

Happy Birthday, Jesus
Forever in our hearts
Forever in our thoughts and prayers
Happy Birthday, Jesus

The Week Before Christmas

'Twas the week before Christmas
And all through the house
There was laughing and hollering
No one could even hear a mouse

Because all the schools were closed
We kids were home for two weeks
And for crying out loud
Mom and Dad could not go to sleep

As I walked carefully through the house
The presents were not wrapped as I could see
Then I thought and wondered
Just which ones were meant for me

The next few days were frustrating
While the presents were placed under the tree with care
I bit my nails with anticipation
Then I saw the sign which said "BEWARE"

It said not to open the presents
Before the assigned time
So I tip-toed back to my bedroom
Hoping not to be seen doing a crime

Each present had a tear
Was it me trying to get a peek?
Well maybe yes or maybe no
I just wanted to sneak

The day of Christmas finally arrived
And my curiosity got the better of me
I unwrapped each gift
And realized how blessed I must be

Christmas Eve

It was the night before Christmas
And all through the house
Not a creature was stirring
Not even a teenager with an IPOD

All the stockings were hung
By the fireplace with care
In hopes that Santa would be there
And hoping to bring some products for my hair

When all of a sudden
I heard a loud clatter (thought it was squirrels)
I went to the garage
To get a ladder (me on a ladder?)

I climbed up so quietly
To see the cause
To my surprise I saw the man himself
Santa Claus (he does exist)

He was dressed in red
And looked rather dashing
I even saw a red light
That was constantly flashing

No, there were not any reindeer
Nor sleigh and bells either
But what to my surprise
A pretty cool helicopter (I know it doesn't rhyme with anything)

He moved over to our chimney with silence and grace
So I stealthily moved back down the ladder
To get into the house
Yes, it was a race

He spoke not a word
But quickly opened his sack
Then all of a sudden he saw me
And said, "I'll be right back"

He didn't go up the chimney
But opened the front door and walked outside
My eyes flew open with surprise and glee
I saw in the driveway a 1968 Corvette Stingray
Just for me (my dream car)

And with that done he suddenly
Left out of sight
But not until he said,
"Merry Christmas to all and
To all a Good Night"

Two Days after Christmas

T'was two days after Christmas
And all through the house
Toys and paper were scattered
Did I just see a mouse?

All the stockings were still hung
By the fireplace with care
Is that Santa I hear
Snoring in my reclining chair?

What is OK by me
Is leftovers again for dinner
Because it always
Tastes to me like a winner

When all of a sudden
My dog barks for me to come here
Oh my goodness! Look in the backyard
Anyone can see all of Santa's reindeer

I rushed in the house
And woke Santa from a deep snore
He quickly hooked his reindeer to the sleigh
Then he said something and began to soar

As he rose above the rooftops
Santa began to holler,
"Merry Christmas to all
No stop! That's really
Happy New Year, Ya'll"

The Day after Easter

"Twas the day after Easter
And all through the house
There were creatures stirring
Including a mouse

The Easter eggs were stuffed
And eaten with zest
Even though the ham and sweet potatoes
Tasted the Best

The kids were up, dressed,
And ready for school
Mom and Dad were ready for work
All was cool

Now everything is back to "normal"
And Easter has come and gone
Remember what Easter is all about
With Jesus nothing will go wrong

Romance

Cards of Love

Mother's Day, Father's Day
A birthday or two
Christmas and Easter
An anniversary saying, "I Love You"

Gifts are normally given
And flowers can be sent
But nothing can compare
To the cards that we get

Cards are emotions
From words of the heart
They can be given hand-to-hand
Or from miles apart

Sometimes they are handwritten
Other times they are not
But nothing can compare
To the cards we get and got

The Heart of a Cowboy

Wyatt Earp he's not
But he's got the heart of a cowboy
Ponderosa is not his home
But the open range is his church
When he praises God daily

A cowboy's heart is true and pure
But sometimes he's lonely
Even though he dearly loves his horse
However the search for a true cowgirl
Continues and is reached with God's love

As the cowboy rides away
He is guided towards his true destiny
With the love of God in their hearts
The two ride together seeking a sunrise
So they can begin a love to last forever and ever

Look into My Eyes

I look into your eyes
And see the windows to your soul
I hear your voice
And it is music to my ears
Your laughter knocks
On my heart's door
What message do I perceive?

Now look into my eyes
And see the happiness light up
Listen to my voice
And hear the generation of love
My heart is opening the door
And is receiving answers to questions

As we look into each other's eyes
We already know what to see
As we have a conversation with each other
We already know what the topic is about
As our hearts make a continuous beat
They are beating as one

As I Look Into Your Eyes

As I look into your eyes
I realize that words are not needed
A simple gesture such as a kiss
Can speak hundreds of words

While we hold each other's hands
We feel the spark of love
Traveling throughout our bodies
Straight from the heart

Our love for each other is genuine
Because we both know it's a miracle
So as we travel into the future
Let's always cherish what we have

Searching

My lips say, "I love you"

Whose ears are listening?

My eyes are searching the skies

Whose eyes are looking back?

My arms are outstretched

Whose arms are hugging back?

My heart aches for that special someone

Whose heart is beating my name?

My love is strong and rich

Whose love reaches my heart?

My thoughts are filled with hope

Whose thoughts are in sync?

The Key

In your hands
You hold the key
To my heart

The key in your hands
Holds what true love is
So the mystery ends

The key unlocks super love
A love that has been hidden
And now it soars

A love which will last
Forever and ever
Into eternity it shall be

For the discovery of such love
Shall be forever
And shall never end

A Moment in Time

A Cinderella moment
When time stands still
One night, one kiss, a magic moment
Wishes for eternity

Dreams caressed
Within your lovin' arms
Reaching out for that star
Love is in the air
And I grasp it with all my might
Hoping to fill my heart

The morning sun shines in your eyes
As I gaze at you with delight
Sweet kisses of joy
Fill my head with happiness
Lifting my heart to ecstasy
Fulfilling my dreams of hope

In My Dreams

In my dreams
I can kiss your lips
And stroke your face

In my dreams
I look into your eyes
And see the love
Of a special connection

In my dreams
We are laughing
And tickling each other

In my dreams
We enjoy each other
And are having fun

In my dreams
I am holding you
As if to never let you go

In my dreams
I know you are close
No matter how far you are

All things come true
If only in my dreams

The Point of Dreaming

What's the point of dreaming

When dreams don't come true

What's the point of dreaming

When I can't be with you

What's the point of dreaming

When I'm not kissing or holding you

So tell me to throw

Out these doubts and thoughts

And I'll know that all

My dreams will be caught

COVID does not equal LOVE

I long to look at your smile
But I can't see it
I long to feel your kiss
But can't experience it
I long to hear "I love you"
But cannot listen to it

There's a mask in the way
I long to yank it off your face
But I'm unable to touch it
So what's the answer?
Your touch or the Mask?

I long for your touch
But we can't hold hands
There is a barrier before us
It is called quarantine or loneliness

I yearn for your hugs
But hate being 6' away
I feel like reaching out
And grabbing you anyway

I want to touch your cheek
But there's a mask in the way
I want to hold and kiss you
So the Mask will just have to go.

God's Plan

While sitting in church one day
I close my eyes and pray
Then with a gentleness and hope attached
I feel an arm placed upon my shoulders

This gesture feels so complete and loving
Do I dare to open my eyes
To see who surrounds me with care
I simply wait for God to give me an answer

As I complete my prayers and thank yous
Gently but slowly my eyes open
However I am still looking down at my feet
Then God directs me to look next to me at you

As we look into each other's eyes and smile
God has moved us to this moment
Your arm around me to make sure of the smiles
That complete the beating of our hearts together

I Close My Eyes

I close my eyes and feel a dream
I see you looking down at me
You gently put my chin in your hand
Softly, I feel a kiss on my lips

Do I dare wake up and
Discover an untruth
Or do I keep my eyes closed
And relish the dream

My heart flutters for a moment
As if to suddenly stop
My eyes remain closed
To savor the feeling that I have

I struggle to wake up
But my mind says, NO
Then I hear a noise
And wake up to see the truth

SO WHAT IS THE TRUTH?

I'd Rather Close My Eyes

I'd rather close my eyes
And see you are here
Instead of opening them
And see you are not

I'd rather close my eyes
And kiss your lips
Instead of opening them
And not feel your mouth

I'd rather close my eyes
And feel your touch
Instead of opening them
And feel absolutely nothing

I'd rather close my eyes
And make sweet love with you
Instead of opening them
To see you are not there

I'd rather close my eyes
And touch and feel and kiss you
Instead of opening them
To see only air

Forever Love

Invisible lover; Invisible heart
I pray we never part
I can't see you with my eyes
But I feel your kisses through the sky

Although we have never met
My love for you is all set
Two hearts in love beat as one
That's how we are, my dear hon

Our love grows each and every day
And no one shall get in our way
Miles between us are not few
But our love is still new

I feel I've known you for years
As I feel joy through tears
I long to hold you close to me
So we can forever be

You're Never Too Old to be Young

Holding Hands while walking
Sneaking a kiss or two
Sleeping together 'til noon
You're never too old to be young

Shopping for groceries can be fun
Looking into each other's eyes
Feeling the love for each other
You're never too old to be young

Remembering the good ole days
While dancing to songs on the radio
Giving "just because" gifts of the heart
You're never too old to be young

Love letters sent and received
Sharing recipes and sharing hugs
Stroking each other's gray hair
You're never too old to be young

Seasonal

Texas Weather

God is laughing: Ha – Ha – Ha
At all the weathermen across the state
When thunder and rain is predicted
Then suddenly the sun peeks out
And when hot weather is on the rise
Then sure enough it rains
Only in Texas is the weather
Like a Rollercoaster
One day it's 90 degrees
And the next it's in the 70s
Rollercoaster, rollercoaster
Texas weather
YES!

Football and Jerseys

High School Friday night lights
Along with college afternoon delights
High school, college, NFL ball
How great they are all

But what about little league
Well, just sit down and enjoy the scene
Hot dogs, popcorn, and soda too
Nothing like enjoying football food

Jerseys are the clothes players wear
They can handle a punch, dirt, and a tear
Push and shove and tackles too
Your team didn't win? Boo Hoo Hoo!

Half time can be lots of fun
From playing horns to beating drums
Halftime dancers are called Drill Team
And all-in-all fans can even scream

From the first whistle to the last
Watching football can be such a blast

Spring is Springing

Spring is Springing
Grass is greening
Birds are singing
Trees are saying "Alleluia"

Bees are buzzing
Mowers are whirring
Weed eaters are humming
Ahhhh fresh mowed grass

Spring cleaning is beginning
Vendor sales on the move
New beginnings on the horizon
Shedding bad habits

Graduations are being planned
Looking forward to a vacation
Whether it be a cruise
Or a trip to the coast

Spring is springing
Are you ready
Shed the cold weather
Cherish the colors

The Voice of Flowers

They have no mouth, but seem to speak
A thousand words so mild and meek.

They have no eyes, but seem to see
And bury thoughts into me.

They have no ears, but seem to hear
All my cries, my every tear.

Grow a few and then you'll know
How your life is fresh and new.

With a smile so broad, I thank my God,
Whose work to imagine is really too hard.

The Prescence of Summer

Winter and Spring have hit the trail
With rain then flowers and leaves on the rise
No more tornados or wild winds
Now it's time for summer to step in
Whether it's swimming, cruises, or the beach
Vacations are planned for fun
So, let's hit the road
Whether a plan, train, bus, or car
A destiny is in the wind
Anticipation for a road trip or a Caribbean Cruise
Or just laying in the sun by a pool
Yes, Summer is here
And it's about time too!!!!

Religious

My Father in Heaven

To my Father in Heaven
I am shouting my love for You
Throwing all doubts away
Feeling Your arms around me

To my Father in Heaven
I give You all my fears
Wherever I look or walk
Your presence is forever with me

To my Father in Heaven
I lift up my happiness
As well as my depression
You are always with me

Reaching Out

(as told to Glenda by our Lord Jesus Christ)

It takes a weary heart to fall apart
It takes a pair of eyes to see a disguise
It takes a pair of feet to walk away

Sooooo

Bring your heart into My arms
And open your eyes
Then take your feet and walk My way

It takes a pair of ears to not hear My words
It takes a pair of hands to wave goodbye
It takes a pair of arms to be uncharmed

Soooooo

Open up your ears and listen to My words
Reach out with your hands and arms
To know and never forget
I   LOVE   YOU

Misc.

Odd to Scott

Now that you are eighteen
What decisions will you make
From playing GI Joe to being in the Army
What adventures will you take

From bicycles to fast cars
Does it seem so long ago
When you were getting muddy
And going on your first date

Ten years ago you were eight
Without a care in the world
Now that you're grown and a man
All the cares in the world will be yours

But as you look back and ponder
Don't forget how to laugh and cry
Don't forget all those who care
And those who say they are proud

(Dedicated to one of my former students, Scott)

Ode to Balls

Some balls bounce
Some can be thrown
Some are kicked
While others are hit

There are baseballs
As well as soft ones too
Which are thrown or caught
And hit to make homeruns

What about bowling balls
Weighing as much as
A sack of potatoes
Boy! Are they heavy

There are large balls
Such as a basket balls
There are small balls too
Often found on a golf course

Balls, balls, everywhere
No matter where you are
Balls are used by everyone
No matter how small or tall

Balls on the play ground
Balls in a gym
Balls on a diamond
Balls in the air

No matter the sport
Or game you are playing
Balls can be seen
And are most definitely fun

So if whether you are two
Or the young age of ninety
Pick up a ball; toss it around
And just have some laughs and fun

A True Friend

Friends may come – and friends may go
But a true friend hangs around forever
I'll be there when you're sad
Or when things get really bad
I'll even be there when you're super glad
I'll hang around when you're angry and sore,
So don't worry about opening my door;
For I don't care how things seem to be
Because I'll always want you to lean on me.

FRIENDS

The Catalytic Converter Problem

When out on the lawn there rose such a clatter
I sprang from the bed to see what was the matter
Away to the window I flew like a flash
Tore open the shutters and threw open the sash

The Catalytic Converter made a loud scream
This was made by a saw that sounded mean
And to my surprise three millennials came out from under my van
And between all three there was not one man

The next two days all was silent around this car
Not a sound can be heard neither close nor far
Then all of a sudden a siren was heard
So loud that I thought it was shrieking birds

As I rushed outside to see what caused the sound
I soon found out that it was a cat for crying out loud
So I took a broom and swept under my van
And finally the sneaky cat began to scram

Silence is Golden

Heard some noise down the hall
Made by young'uns;
Mom gave birth to all
The hollering was loud indeed
She began to roll her eyes
Then she began to grit her teeth
Mom then hollered back with a blast
Y'all be quiet if you please
And all of a sudden her voice was last
There was no sound to be heard, none at all
Mom sat and pondered; her ear was bent
The suddenly she sailed quickly down the hall
Because the children were too silent
And Mom must find out why

Bottom line: Silence is Golden or Is it?

The Good Ole Days

Remember when girls wore poodle skirts
And boys did not wear jeans
Pony tails were popular for just girls
But guys had to wear short hair

Remember saddle oxfords and penny loafers
Plus tennis shoes were worn for PE
Friday night lights meant HS football
Afterwards there was the victory dance

Remember riding bicycles around the hood
Was not only safe but accepted
Playing cops and robbers on the bikes
And using playing cards to make it like a motorcycle

Remember manners were accepted
And saying Yes ma'am and Yes sir
Throwing in Please and Thank you
Came automatically out of the mouths of kids

Remember standing up for pledges in school
And bowing heads for prayer
Lunches in the cafeteria were delicious
However sack lunches were kinda good too

Remember going to church on Sunday
And wearing our best dresses or suits
Afterwards we all sat down for family lunch
Bowing our heads to say grace

As you travel back in time and remember
Never forget your memories
And always, yes always
Remember the good ole days

Gabby Lee aka Glenda Jensen is a retired English teacher who attributes her imaginative and creative writing to the many family stories that her grandparents told her while she was growing up. Not only family has inspired her to write but also her former students. She also gives some credibility to her own imagination while growing up whether it is playing cowboys and Indians with her neighbors using bicycles as horses or pretending to swing through the jungles on a swing set. Glenda is currently a freelance writer who also has had two poems and several novels published.

Glenda currently resides in Mesquite, Texas along with her husband, John, and his dog, Abbey.. She is the mother of three grown children, six grandchildren, and great grandchildren who also have been an inspiration for her writing.

www.ingramcontent.com/pod-product-compliance
Lightning Source LLC
Chambersburg PA
CBHW050904120626
46554CB00003B/997